EIGHT WAYS
to Lift
YOUR *Spirit*

christine martin

Unless otherwise indicated, all Scripture quotations are taken from the King James Version.

Eight Ways to Lift Your Spirit
ISBN 0-9700987-2-3
Copyright 2001 by Christine Martin

Published by Favor International
P.O. Box 608150
Orlando, Florida 32860

Acknowledgements

Well, where do I start?

I first want to say thank you to my God, for having patience with this cute, little, messed-up, New York girl! I made it, or should I say I am making it. I have a long way to go, but I have come a long way! This life is a journey, and I am happy to say I am enjoying the trip.

There have been many obstacles in my way, but I have determination and a fight for survival. I have a God who loves me enough to have never left me. Thanks, God, for waiting for my recognition of you, stepping into my life to rescue me and lift my spirit. My Life will never be the same. I will Love you always. — Your chosen, Christine.

Aside from God, I want to say thank you to the other three great men in my life. To My Dad…your love and support helped mold me into the woman I am today. Your strict ways, and yet loving heart, strengthened me in more ways than I could ever explain. I am proud to call you my dad. Your faith in me will never go unnoticed! Loving you till the day I die. Thanks DAD! Christine

To my little (BIG) brother, Len… thanks for your friendship that has always been an encouragement when I needed it most.

And to the man I have waited for all my life…my husband, Dave! Your love has been a breath of fresh air to my life. I admire your ability to stand and succeed even when others mocked and said you would fail!!! This has taught me that I, too, can stand and be a success. I have learned so much from your example. Thank you for pushing me to succeed and to write this book, you're right… I feel great! We made it baby, didn't we? My love is yours forever. Your wife, Christine.

Acknowledgements

To my mother...words are not enough! Thanks for never giving up on me, even when I put you through hell! LOOK MOM, I really did it!

To my sister April...Hey, Staples this is a far cry from slinging burgers isn't it? HAHAHA! I love you and thank you for your servant's heart in my life. You are a precious gift that I will always treasure.

To the rest of my family, you know who you are...From the bottom of my heart, I thank you for believing in this once messed-up girl. Thank God for change, huh!

My friends, who are definitely few but absolutely REAL, thanks for your love and support!

Last, but not least, to all those back-stabbing, so-called friends (and even enemies) who thought and said that I would never make it and never amount to anything...I Love you anyway! I thank you with much gratitude for pushing me to be a success and for letting me realize I had great potential. You were just jealous of what I didn't even see in me at the time! THANKS A BUNCH!! Your enemy is only proof that you have a future. If it were not so they wouldn't bother to try so hard to take you down!!!

Why I Wrote This Book

I can think of numerous occasions when I felt down and out... when I thought the entire world had left me, even God. I felt as if all my creativity had been lost, even the energy and excitement of living had been sucked out of my life. I remember times when I would sit and cry and wonder when this season would change for me. How long would it last, and where is my breakthrough?

I felt like this little, lost girl in search of not only answers to these questions but in search of her significance. Well, I definitely found my answers as well as my significance. It was when I realized God never really left me. He was always there to guide me, to give me peace. I found a strength that came from deep within my soul; a strength and confidence of knowing everything would be all right. This strength only came from my God.

I wrote this book so that you will be uplifted and that your confidence level in who you are will be uplifted and to let you know that with God ALL things are possible. You can have a lifted spirit, even if you feel like yours is crushed right now. I encourage you to keep reading and DON'T GIVE UP!

If you have ever felt alone, discouraged, lost, without guidance, and without creativity...then read on. This book is just for you. My prayer is that, as you read this book, a freedom will come over you, the joy that you lost will be restored, and your body, soul, mind and spirit will be lifted. There lies within each and every one of us a fight for survival, to win and to conquer. You will regain what has been lost as your mind is filled with the thoughts and revelations in the pages ahead of you. STAY FOCUSED. Read on...*and enjoy!*

Table of Contents

Chapter		Page
1	Give It to God	*9*
2	When I Know, I Grow	*15*
3	Develop a Right Attitude	*21*
4	Get Your Stuff in Order	*35*
5	Spoil Yourself	*41*
6	Mirror, Mirror on the Wall	*47*
7	Seasons Change	*53*
8	Get Your Directions from Upstairs	*57*

Give it
to God

CHAPTER ONE

Give it to God

I have had countless occasions and opportunities set before me to give it to God. I mean situations that I knew I couldn't handle on my own...crisis that had hit the heart of my family and only God could intervene. However, I learned the hard way on how to do what I am explaining to you right now...Give It To God! Sounds easy, huh? Well, I do hope as I share with you in this chapter personal stories of tragedies and triumphs on how to give it to God, you will learn from my mistakes. There are two ways one can learn...by mistakes and by mentors. I urge you, if you relate to anything you are about to embark on in this book, then take it from me...learn. Why repeat the same test twice? Study, and pass the first time.

How many times have you said, "I will leave this at the feet of Jesus? I will not battle with this. I do not have all the answers. I choose to be victorious and overcome. Therefore, God take over!" Then just a few hours later (ok, maybe for some of you it was a few days later...) you picked the problem back up. *Hello...what are you thinking?* We do ourselves an injustice when we cast all our cares on Him and then retrieve them back into our own arms again. Silly, Silly...when do we learn?

The Bible tells us that if we are weary and heavy burdened, we can come to Jesus and He will give us rest. It also says lean not to your own understanding, but in all of your ways to acknowledge Him. I don't know about you, but there have been many times when I made God and His Word so entirely complicated. I know that you know, as well as me, what we are supposed to do. So, if God has given us all these promises in His Word, tells us He cares for us and wants us to be victorious, then don't you think we should just take His Word for what it is worth and give Him our concerns, worries, etc...?

I would hate to think that God is up there saying, "Christine, I have all the answers. This is a TEST and only a TEST. Please give it to me and all will be well." Sometimes I think God is up there saying, "OH Brother, I created that, the poor, little thing. I knew exactly what she would go through, and I have all the answers." No, God would never say that. I just think that sometimes, haven't you?

What do I mean when I say we are doing ourselves an injustice? I mean that we cause wrong to come to us when Jesus makes it right. We may cause ourselves to have fear, anxiety and worry (call it what you may), but we allow these emotions to stay close to us when we don't release it to God. Make use of your troubles. Cast it onto Jesus and learn. A lot of times I have found that even in the midst of chaos I have gained strength. It built character in me and taught me to resist the devil. He *will* flee from me. I have learned that things are temporary. Friends may change, your job may change, but Jesus NEVER changes. He is always the same, and He wants only the best for us!

It really is to our benefit when we realize that there may be some things we are dealing with that are results of "NOT" giving it to God. I do believe (and this is my belief from my own personal studies of the Word and my own experiences) that God knows all things, and there may be situations He allows only to build us and mold us. However, I think sometimes that the reason crisis or concerns may be magnified in our life is because we choose to hold it all in. We choose to figure it out, and we choose to become bitter, angry, hurt, maybe even rejected and the list goes on.

We have a choice in life, and the Word tells us to choose "life" so we can have it more abundantly. We have a choice to give it to God and allow Him to be our strength, our peace, and our comforter…to allow God to have His way in His timing and work things on our behalf. Remember the choice of victory or defeat is ours. Which one do you choose?

I have learned from many people whom I have dealt with in counseling (or just on a friend-to-friend basis) that we can at times become our worst enemy. I understand that people are mean at times, and tend to say awful things that can be hurtful. For example, a spouse chooses to leave, you lose a job leaving you to find another place of employment, your child says he hates you or a friend betrays you. I do not know your battle today, but I do know that I have a friend who knows all the answers, and His name is Jesus. He will never leave you nor forsake you, although it may feel like it sometimes. Just do the following:

1 STOP finding fault in all you do and what others do.

2 REGROUP — take time to breathe and think.

3 DO NOT act out of emotions.

4 GO to a quite place and call on the name of Jesus.

Jesus is waiting to hear your cry of surrender. Your heart belongs to Him, so allow Him to mend it and give you your answers as YOU give it to GOD! I know it may not be easy, because we want to give a list of who has done us wrong, and why these bad things happen. "...If only so and so wouldn't have done this, then I would never have said that..." Well, we are not to judge others. We are only held accountable for ourselves.

The Bible says to do unto others, AS you would have them do unto you...not necessarily saying they would be nice or would be kind unto you. The Bible says just AS you would want them to act, to give of yourself in a kind and loving matter regardless of what others say or how they treat you, is a much greater law. This law is the law of LOVE. It is the law of forgiveness that brings healing, confidence and peace. It is a wonderful thing when we can give it to God and still Love.

> *Give of yourself in a kind and loving matter regardless of what others say, or how they treat you.*

I remember a time in my life when I had been betrayed so badly, and all I wanted to do was defend myself. I wanted everyone to know who was to blame for this situation. Still to this day the truth of the matter may never be known. But, I don't care, because I gave it to God! God knows the truth, and the truth shall set you free. The freedom of knowing I was right (and didn't defend myself) is great! It showed a maturing in Christ. It showed that I could survive, and caused me to really love my enemy. Did it hurt? Oh YEAH! I shared with you my initial response. I may have been being a bit passive because I was really thrown for a loop at the cause of this crisis and who was really at fault. I was utterly shocked at who was involved and who had been deceived by this

lie. I do not feel it is necessary to give a complete description of this event, but I will tell you that I found out who my real friends were and about their "real personality." I, also, found out that Jesus truly is a friend that sticks closer than a brother.

All I can really say to you is that I understand what it is like to want to be the avenger, but remember Romans 12:19b, *"...vengeance is mine saith the Lord."* It took me many obstacles and many stories to tell of how I have learned to give it to God. I will share more detail as you read. I believe the truth of the matter is lying within each and every one of us. We know deep down what is the right thing to do. As "Nike" so simply states it: *Just Do It!* Just do the right thing.

Keep your head up high, and give it to God. The bottom line is…when life becomes hard and days become dim, don't struggle, worry, fret or try to cope all alone. Put all the situations in God's hands, trusting that He knows what is best for you and for everyone else involved in this world. Just give it to God!

When I Know, I Grow

CHAPTER TWO

When I Know, I Grow

With knowledge comes responsibility, with responsibility we need wisdom. With wisdom comes success, and with success we obtain achievement and joy which lifts our spirits.

Wisdom is one of life's most valuable keys to success. It will keep you if you follow its instruction. Having wisdom will increase your ability to have self-confidence and lift your spirits. From business deals, to the stock market, to running a family, wisdom is a very crucial part of our life and should be applied to our every decision.

"My people are destroyed for lack of knowledge."
(HOSEA 4:6)

"If any of you lack wisdom, let him ask of God, that giveth to all men liberally, and upbraideth not; and it shall be given him." (JAMES 1:5)

Wisdom, in the Greek is "sophia", cleverness; skill; scientific knowledge, wisdom. God is no respecter of persons, and as it is obvious in the book of James, He will give liberally to those who ask. Wisdom is a matter of renewing the mind. It is the heart of God that one should desire. To think the way God thinks and to act in a manner of His character is truly an asset to who we are in Him.

What one loves can be determined in what he asks for. When we have mixed up priorities and bad attitudes our decision making is fogged. Our ability to have a positive outlook on life, and view it with clarity, is hard to do. You must have wisdom in order to have a healthier you.

This may sound strange to you, but it is the simple things in life we tend to over look that can really make a big difference. With wisdom it is easy to develop a positive you, a positive outlook on things, and to have clarity and peace of mind in your entire decision making. This clarity will bring an ease about things — a joy — and will definitely lift your spirit because you will have a sense of success that comes from wisdom.

The things you know help you grow. They help shape you or break you. It is better to have wisdom and make mistakes along the way than to be an ignorant person and die without ever trying to succeed. Wisdom is the simple statement that is so profound. Have you ever heard any one speak one or two words that impacted an entire statement or even helped alter your life in a dramatic way? It is wiser to keep your mouth shut, if you do not have the answer or solution to a problem, rather than to babble and go on endlessly without any intent. This is ignorance.

Wisdom is discreet. In Proverbs 31:26, the passage of scripture is the countenance of the virtuous woman. *"She openeth her mouth with wisdom; and in her tongue is the law of kindness."* This woman is wise. She speaks with intelligence and cleverness. She is cultured in mind and manners. Notice here how wisdom is linked to the mind. Romans 12:2 reflects the importance of renewing the mind, which constitutes the perfect and acceptable will of God. Some people walk around defeated, not realizing the potential and the ability that lies within them. If they were to ask God, their Father in Heaven for wisdom, they would be set free.

It is better to seek God's Hand of provision for all your needs than the earthy possessions that will not even perfect our happiness. For if a man has wisdom, he can possess far more things and have better clarity in situations. It is easier to have clear-cut goals, and increase when we seek and search out wisdom. The nature of wisdom needs to be in the heart of every individual seeking to become more like God — more of a success, and more of a great leader.

Whether you are the president of a company, a CEO, a banker, a car salesman, a truck driver, or a homemaker, you can still possess wisdom and still be a success to your fullest potential. It is all up to you. Do you seek wisdom or not? Luke 12:34 says, *"For where your treasure is, there will your heart be also."* If anyone has his heart towards the riches of this earth, it is evident what reward he will receive. Where lack of wisdom is concerned, one can run into masses of problems when the proper counsel is not advised. There is wisdom in the multitude of counsel. Seed, which will reap proficient harvest, can be sown with wise advice.

"But the wisdom that is above is first pure then peaceable, gentle, and easy to be entreated, full of mercy and good fruits, without partiality and without hypocrisy." (JAMES 3:17)

This verse in James describes the characteristics of divine wisdom — the characteristics one should follow after. The first characteristic is *purity*, which is clean and just. If the thoughts are pure, then the mind is at ease…for every good and perfect thing comes from God. Therefore purity is of good virtue. It will keep you.

Peaceable, another characteristic of Divine Wisdom. Hebrews 12:14 says, *"Follow peace with all men, and holiness, without which no man shall see the Lord."* This is a command by God to follow peace. Follow in the Greek "dioko" means to pursue, chase, and seek after…which are the same reasons to obtain wisdom — to follow after God to seek and to pursue His heart. "Gentle" meaning meek, modest and kind, is incorporated in divine wisdom. To be entreated is yielding to others. When one yields to another, they give heed to what is being said and done. A definite characteristic to make a wise decision is to yield. Fully equipped with mercy and good fruits is the law of kindness, the active part of divine wisdom.

Looking at the end of verse 17, we see that there is no partiality. This means no respecter of person — the trait also of God. One without hypocrisy, being open, genuine, true and honest. These all define the characteristics of divine wisdom, as it is evident these are the characteristics of God, the Father, also. When one has divine wisdom, they have the heartbeat of God. They have true humility. *True humility will lift your spirits.*

You are a clean vessel, a well-run ship, and you know you are doing the very best you can with what you've been given. This will lift your spirits just knowing you tried. As a vessel whose mind is polluted with garbage, this is a vessel that will, in turn, become a poor leader. Wisdom and knowledge creates a good, strong leader — a morally and spiritually effective ambassador, ready for the front line.

"Wisdom is supreme; therefore get wisdom. Though it cost all you have, get understanding." (PROVERBS 4:7; NEW INT'L VERSION)

Wisdom is the ability to make use of knowledge effectively.

Dr. Myles Munroe states, "Wisdom is the ability to make use of knowledge effectively." Wisdom is more precious than rubies, and nothing you desire can compare with it. There are many people who may have *information*, but they have no *revelation*. People perish for lack of knowledge. They have not obtained the power of God or the source of God.

There are many intellectual qualifications an individual must obtain. One great quality all must possess is "Wisdom", in its higher ability to enable us to become all that we have been created to be. Our mind is a powerful tool. Without the wisdom of God, and His heartbeat, we are but immature vessels wandering aimlessly to fulfill a potential we have not yet tapped into. Wisdom is a combination of discernment, judgment and tact. When God's mind becomes imparted in to us through His wisdom, we have success.

It is a challenge everyday to walk as the desired vessel we were created to be. Yet with God all things are possible. To imagine a world where wisdom is not exemplified is to have a world without order and structure. The keys lie within our hand. The wisdom to grasp is all up to the individual. If one seeks, he finds. If he knocks, the door shall be opened. The choice is entirely up to you — a world of ignorance or a lifestyle of obedience? You choose. But, may I suggest you choose wisdom. Choose to be wise in all your endeavors.

Creating true success and a happy mind full of wisdom will lift your spirits. You will soar to new heights as you travel this journey of life.

Develop A
Right Attitude

CHAPTER THREE

Develop A Right Attitude

"You can't be a smart cookie if you have crummy attitude"

"Your attitude determines your altitude"

These are statements that we have all heard before. What does the word *attitude* mean? It means a bodily posture showing mood, action, etc.; a manner showing one's feelings or thoughts; one's disposition, opinion, etc.

Attitude is everything, and it affects everything.

Your attitude today will determine your success tomorrow.

You have the ability, the know how, to revolutionize your life and soar to the peaks of success and fulfillment. Whether your attitude is positive, negative or just somewhere in between, I believe this chapter will help you view *attitude* in a new perspective as it did me when I first began to study this subject. You will learn how to take control of your thought patterns, turn your mind over to God and unleash your incredible potential.

This is a touchy subject because so many times we think our attitude does not need adjustments. OK, maybe not you, so just pass this on to someone you know who needs an attitude adjustment! Seriously, we need to recognize what is keeping us from having a good attitude. We must interrogate ourselves with questions such as:

▶ *Why am I having a bad day?*

▶ *What has caused my emotions to flare up?*

▶ *What is the "real" root of the problem I am battling?*

▶ *Would Jesus act this way?*

▶ *What does the Word say about how I should act?*

There are many equations that determine our attitudes, good or bad, but how we choose to react toward them is a different story. Our attitude should be pleasing to God.

For many people, a good attitude will be accompanied by their faith and walk with God while others will believe that nothing follows death — but, oh well...they gave it their best shot. I believe it's taking the time to smell the roses and enjoy a walk in the park. Enjoy your life and count the blessings instead of listing the pains and miseries. It is the willingness to fight against all odds, but also willingness to accept any consequences.

Finally, it is the determination to love and appreciate every moment the eyes take in light, the ears take in sound and the lungs take in air.

Ok, here's another question to interrogate yourself with. *Can a good attitude be learned?* I believe that with some effort, and the desire to change, it can. Remember change is inevitable, but misery is optional. A "positive attitude" can be considered a philosophy. A philosophy requires a faith in the correctness of the beliefs, and just as we believe in God, our faith takes action and works in our behalf. It is more than just memorizing some lines out of a book. You have to believe and understand the truths of the words. The Word of God tells us that life and death are in the power of the tongue.

The way we view our circumstances is often determined by our mouth and actions. We have choices. Again, I strongly believe we can focus on the negative and make our body sick, or we can focus on the positive and bring energy and enthusiasm into our being. Either way, the choice is up to you. Allow God to work on the inside of you.

If all you have known while growing up is negativity and defeat then your mind may need to be reconditioned by the renewing of God's Word and prayer. However, this is no excuse to be lazy in your thinking and say I cannot change. This is how I grew up. Hog Wash! You can change! I did, and I still work on my attitude. In fact, I think it is an ongoing process that can only be determined by the time we spend renewing our mind and feeding ourselves positive thoughts daily! Bad habits can be broken.

Did you ever realize how hard it is to start a diet or an exercise program? You know, something that was "good" for you and would cause a positive reaction in your health. Then the day came when you made a firm decision to start after weeks of procrastination and saying, "I'll do it tomorrow..." Your program begins, you feel motivated, energized and extremely positive. Then a friend invites you out to a birthday celebration, or a family vacation comes up and all you see is an opportunity to EAT! Oh, it's only one day, and you say to yourself, "This won't hurt. Besides I have been so good for the last four days...I can cheat once." Before you know it you are off your diet and back to feeling yucky, speaking the negative. All those around you notice your attitude has plummeted.

All I can say is see how hard it was to start your program? How you had to work a little harder at gaining a positive attitude and do something healthy for your body? Look how easy it was to break a good habit and postpone your wonderful feeling of achievement, success and a good attitude.

Attitude is a little thing that makes a BIG difference.

We can change our attitude. We just have to make a choice. By the way, if you have stopped your exercise program, now would be a good time to pick it back up and regain your healthy outlook on life…just a thought. Either way you must be happy with you. I just used the diet analogy because it is one I am sure we all can relate to. The main lesson I want you to learn is to keep a good attitude no matter what comes your way.

"God, grant me the serenity to accept the things
I cannot change; courage to change the things I can;
and wisdom to know the difference."
(SERENITY PRAYER, *Dr. Reinhold Niebuhr*)

It is so important that one learns, understands and believes these words. It is just as important as believing in yourself and having faith enough in God that your attitude can change. You will feel great when you allow this process to take place. You have to know when you are slamming yourself mentally against a brick wall and know when to quit it. Please do not beat yourself over the head because you are working on your attitude and it hasn't changed overnight. It did not take you overnight to gain a bad attitude or poor self-image of yourself, so it will not take overnight to fix it. It is a process. So hold on and don't give up!

Happiness and sadness can be dealt with in the same manner. We choose negative or positive thoughts and give them to God in prayer. When something bad happens, a relationship dies, somebody hurts us deeply, or a loved one dies, our emotions are affected. We must know the limit of grief. I understand to cry is normal, and it is okay to shed tears. (God has an account of every tear fallen from your eyes — so I give you permission to cry!)

Good attitudes are important and can be learned. They are achievable if we want them.

I believe there is a grieving period when loss happens in our life. How long should this process last? I cannot answer that. All I can do is tell you this soon shall pass. God is the peace that passes all understanding. He will guard your heart and mind in Christ Jesus. The point I want to stress in this chapter is that good attitudes are important and can be learned. They are achievable if we want them.

26

Ecclesiastes 3 puts it so well, *"...to everything there is a time and season."* We have to know time, and know when we are being ridiculous and throwing ourselves a pity party causing everyone to feel bad for us...thus becoming manipulative. Know when to say no more to this and put a limit on it. I will touch more on this subject in Chapter Five on changing seasons.

Let it all out...your fears, regrets, and sorrow. Feel your releases. Get in touch with your true feelings about an issue. Then just let it go. LET IT GO! You do not need it anymore. You are done with it. Go to God in prayer, get in His presence and get revived again! Create a better memory — a happy attitude. Remember the little saying at the beginning of this chapter? Our *attitudes* determine our *altitudes*.

Some people seem to hang on to their misery like they wish they had hung on to some old boyfriend, an old pair of shoes or some joy or happiness. You can learn to let it go because you realize this is necessary according to scripture and before happiness can return. I want you to know something. I want you to understand that no one can go through life without some bad experiences…including myself.

Life is not fair, but we have a God who is. Turn it to Him and experience enchantment. If you just go on with your life and do your very best, with the help of God, you can be happy again. Don't dwell on the bad times and they'll just pass along. Happiness can always be available down the road if you just allow it.

Another lesson on this attitude journey we are on is to learn the importance of laughing. The Bible says that a merry heart does good like a medicine. You need to laugh every day. Read a joke or don't skip the comics in the paper. I personally call my sister, April, and say, "Hey, make me laugh today I really need it!" Before you know it we get on this kick of joking around and acting so silly just like we did when we were in grade school. I love every minute of it. "Hey, Staples: I'm chopping Brock-o-lea!" (This line goes out to my sister!)

Another healthy way to maintain a positive attitude is to develop friendships with funny people. Too many serious, stuffy people can cramp your style. God is cool, and He is fun. So back off all you religious folks...I choose to enjoy life! When holidays, birthdays or special occasions arise, ask your friends or family to buy you gifts of joke books or books of cartoons. A good out-loud laugh each day can do wonders for your attitude. TRUST ME, I live with the "King of Comedy." My husband, Dave, keeps me in literal stitches. He is a trip. Sometimes I have to tell him he is getting carried away. Slow down there buddy — I can only handle one joke at a time!

Ok, again I want to mention tears. That's right. To all you who think crying is for babies, it can be a great stress release. I cry every time I see a sad movie or see someone less fortunate than myself. But, a minute later I might be laughing at some goofy commercial. These things tend to even out with a positive attitude. I cry on my parent's anniversary because I see how their love kept them together this long…30 years and still going. My husband, Dave, says I don't need any excuse to cry. I am a walking faucet. Oh well, I just say that's how God created me. It took me a long time to learn not to use my tears as a manipulative tool. So let me cry. It's really truthful and liberating.

But the manipulation of tears is a whole other chapter. All I can say is that it doesn't work! You just exhaust yourself out of energy, your eyes swell up like basketballs and you feel like a jerk because no one really paid me much attention when I tried this method. It is better to be real and be you, even if you are having a bad day. Learn to develop a good attitude in spite of it all.

If you learn these lessons, believe in them, and believe in yourself, chances are that a positive attitude can be within your grasp. Remember, WITH God ALL things are possible! A little effort and determination on your part may be all that is required to acquire this attitude that might help prolong your life and help others enjoy your company.

You must also develop a good self-image to maintain a positive attitude. A positive attitude is necessary to be successful in con-frontations, just even in every day life. Your body and mind is a thought factory, and it knows when you feel worthy of winning a fight. The stronger your feeling of adequacy and worthiness, the stronger your immune system becomes. The effort to fight becomes that much easier. I don't mean knock-me-down drag outs. I mean mentally fight to win, survive and be all that God has called you to be! The better you feel about yourself, the harder it is to be oppressed. The more you fill yourself up with the Word of God, and seek Godly counsel on how to achieve and maintain a positive outlook on you, the more you will overcome and be victorious. The more you will see that you will not be an easy victim.

Self-esteem sometimes demands that you attack your opponent and keep HIM on the run. Your opponent is Satan. He knows where to hit you where it hurts…when you are down. Most of the time he uses people close to you. The Bible, however, tells us that we cannot be ignorant of his devises. We must become wise and have understanding! If we do not have understanding we can develop a bad attitude.

Let me give you a definition from the Webster's dictionary of *attitude*. It means: a. a negative or hostile state of mind, b: a cocky or arrogant manner. I like this definition. It gets right to the point. We cannot take offense and become hostile. This creates a poor self-image and causes bad days! Do just the opposite and develop strength, perseverance and fight to have a good attitude. You can do it! I believe in you. You know, the longer I live, the more I realize the impact of my attitude in life. To me, attitude is more important than the facts. It is an essential part of living. My attitude will take me to great places, and I can achieve great things.

Attitudes are contagious…*is yours worth catching?*

Your prospects for good health and long life are remarkably dependent upon mental habits learned in childhood. We went over this a few pages back when we talked about learned behavior and how you can change with effort and time. You did not receive false instruction on your attitude overnight. So be patient. In due time you will be converted into a loving, wonderful magnet of greatness …all as a result of a good, positive GODLY attitude! If we have had to live in strife and contentious situations our attitude may really need some major adjustments. But first, we must WATCH OUR WORDS. People all around you are watching you and your ATTITUDE. Attitude is your window to the world. Are you Christ-like?

Maybe you feel weary and need a pick me up. I want to help you. Matthew 11:28 (NIV) says, *"Come unto me, all you who are weary and 'heavy' burdened, and I will give you rest."* Look at these definitions:

1. WEARY - worn out, tired, without zeal
2. HEAVY - hard to lift because of weight. Intense

Are you carrying too much weight on your shoulders at times? I have been guilty of it before. Whether it is the weight of our job, our marriage, our family or our ministry, these weights will pull us down and cause us to have crummy attitudes. We cannot in our own strength lift ourselves. We must learn to STOP and give it to God. When we are worn out and tired we carry things on ourselves that God did not create for us to carry. But He gives us a solution. God can give us REST, and we will be set free! He said, IF you come, I will give you rest. Rest will keep you restored and rejuvenated. You will have a good attitude, and then you can love yourself easier! To be successful, first you have to love yourself. Look at this equation:

Human Equation =	+ ADD LOVE - SUBTRACT HATE
	x MULTIPLY GOOD AND
	/ DIVIDE BETWEEN TRUTH AND ERROR

When we are in God's presence we operate in love. We act right, speak right and LOVE ourselves! We are successful, awesome human beings created in the image and likeness of God Almighty!

When we carry our burdens, live in stress or turmoil, and allow the chaotic things of everyday life to overtake us, we may tend to subtract love, exemplify hate, misuse good and mistake error for truth. This is not God's plan for us. He said to come just as you are. He tells us in His Word to COME into HIS presence for refreshing and peace.

Do not feel guilty for coming to God and resting in His presence. We are not "Super Humans." We are not exempt from life and all the journeys it takes us on. We can have a restored attitude in God's presence.

Eleanor Roosevelt said, "In all our contacts it is probably the sense of being really needed and wanted which gives us the greatest satisfaction and creates the most lasting bond." This is so similar to our relationship with God. We were created for relationship by our Heavenly Father. Relationship gives Him great satisfaction and creates a bond between our Heavenly Father and us! Eleanor Roosevelt not only was the U.S. First Lady, author, speaker, and diplomat, she had a lot of demands on her life. Like many of us — we have demands, too. The statement she made is very profound. If we could learn to take just a moment of each day and set it aside for our relationship with God we would be ahead of things.

Being in God's presence is all we need. We must not forget and become too busy with our own agenda that we carry a miserable attitude because of our lack of communication with God. Have you ever been at the place in your life of working so much, running here and there, trying to meet all of your deadlines, and forget to get refreshed from God's presence? Now would be a good time to start. Get over it. Give it to God and get your attitude back! I believe in you. You can have an attractive, outrageous and fun-loving attitude today. *It all begins with you.*

I have just a few more notes for you on attitude, and then this chapter is over. It's important for you to learn how to manage and control the quality of your life through the power of a positive attitude. If I did not believe so much in our attitude, I would not have spent so much time on this chapter.

Attitude is the foundation and support of everything we do. It is a key element in the process of reaching our destiny and achieving success in our personal and professional lives. I have attended countless seminars, read hundreds of books and articles and listened to hours upon hours of tapes on the subject of self-mastery. Over and over again I find that the key to success is maintaining a positive attitude. In fact, outside of your relationship with God, the most important asset you can possess is a positive attitude toward life.

32

Your attitude is often one of the first things that people notice about you. You may not be able to change your height or your body type, but you can change your attitude. A good, positive attitude is often determined by your self-image. It is not a product of genetics or heredity, but it is an acquired trait that will require proper training.

A key to a good attitude is being happy with the YOU God created! Liking yourself relates to self-image, which is not limited to your physical appearance. Self-image includes the total you — personality, talents, abilities, accomplishments, desires, goals and a spiritual relationship with the Lord.

Your emotional health is rooted strongly in your self-image. Ultimately, your self-image is linked to who you are in Christ Jesus. If you have no relationship with Christ, it will be difficult for you to have a strong, healthy self-image. If you have a relationship with Christ, however, you have accepted the fact that God loved you so much that He sent Jesus to die for your sins so that you could have eternal life (JOHN 3:16).

As Christians, our worth and self-image must flow from Christ Jesus. *We are worthy because He declares us to be worthy.* The person with a good self-image develops a right attitude by having a daily prayer life, speaking positive confessions and by doing the following:

▶ Accepting both the good and the bad in themselves (the missing link may be celebrating the differences in others).

▶ Being open to a relationship with God and with others.

▶ Expressing love freely and willingly, but always within the constraints of God's will.

▶ Being willing to expose their inner most feelings and ideas.

▶ Having confidence of God's ability at work in, and through their life (acknowledging that God is the source of all their abilities and the One who reinforces and undergirds every effort).

▶ Accommodates failures. Learns from them, and moves forward with no regrets.

The person with a positive self-image sees that God, and future growth and development made possible by God, can more than make up for anything missing.

I hope I have given you plenty of information for your mental training. Get ready to see a difference in how you view things when your attitude changes and your self-image is improved. You are created in the image and the likeness of God! Be happy with the YOU He created.

Develop A
Right Attitude

Observation

Four ways on how I can improve my self-image and take action in helping to develop a "right attitude" are:

1 _____

_____

_____

2 _____

_____

_____

3 _____

_____

_____

4 _____

_____

_____

Get Your Stuff In Order

CHAPTER FOUR

Get Your Stuff In Order

ORDER: THE PROPER ARRANGEMENT OF THINGS.

One of the keys to having a lifted spirit and a healthy outlook on life is to have order in your life. When things are out of place, we can become agitated, frustrated or even procrastinate on more important "to do's" because we figure things are already a mess so why bother. Can you relate? Ok, let me give you an example. Did you ever procrastinate on cleaning your closet out because the mess on the floor overwhelmed you? You know…clothes on the floor, one shoe on the bedroom floor and the mate to it somewhere in the closet. Where do I start you say? Somehow, somewhere inside you, you found a way to muster up the energy to create order, and before you knew it you were feeling great! Productive, energized, and feelings of completion and success entered into your mind all because you decided to create order.

I suggest, turn the music up, find an upbeat, catchy tune, and get to work! Music is the rhythm to our soul. Create your atmosphere by your music. Start feeling energized and clean, clean clean! Make the bed, empty the dishwasher, clean the closet empty the trash cans, clean your refrigerator, take action, and watch your spirit lift.

I don't know where you need order in your life, but I have found a good place to start is in your home. First, you have to establish healthy, creative, and energetic feelings all around you. NO, I am not trying to sound new age, or spooky, or twist your feelings like some spiritual guru. These feelings are simply the feelings you experience when you create order, especially when you have started with your haven first.

Your mind is a powerful tool, and when used correctly, you can create a positive flow of thoughts that lift you. One way to do this is to create order. I hate to sound redundant, but I want to drill it into you how important order is in your life, and how easy you can obtain it when you change your thought process and make a decision to do so.

There are numerous ways to create order in your life, but the first step is to recognize where you need it the most and start there. If you were honest with yourself, this would be a good start. Order can help create a sense of balance. It will establish the accurate arrangement of things in our life and set our feet on the paths to victory.

I mentioned above to first create order by starting in your home, your haven. Maybe you keep an "eat off my floor haven"…spotless-at-all-times home. GREAT! I commend you, but maybe your order is peace in your home, with your spouse, children, etc. Maybe your order needs to start from within. Yes, starting with the way you view yourself. Poor self-image will highly affect your outlook on life and lead to disastrous chaos.

Creating order from the inside out is never a bad place to start. Evaluate yourself. This is something I have mentioned throughout this book. Why? Because evaluation is important for growth, change, motivation and determination. When all these attributes work together in your life, your spirits are lifted.

I want to add a few examples, in this chapter, of ways I have created order in my life. I can remember when I looked in the mirror, and all I saw was a "big mess." I saw disorder everywhere I turned, from my closet to the inner doors of my heart. I needed order desperately in my life. I wanted to create it and didn't have a clue on how to get it. I really cared about myself and deep inside wanted to have a sense of completion, productivity and a sense of joy. Well, it all was right before me. Start one step at a time.

I do not want you to get overloaded and burdened down on creating order. This book is to help lift your spirits…not bury them. So take baby steps to advancement. Besides, when you try to change too many things at once, you're not effective. I used the house cleaning scenario as my personal example because I love nothing better than to come home to a neat house. I feel that when I have a clean home, I can easily relax with a cup of coffee, crawl up onto my bright blue couch with my fluffy zebra blanket, and just relax! I have a good sense of completion and order. I did, however, learn the hard way. That is why I use this cleaning analogy so often.

Let's say I start to clean the bathroom. I am on my way to order. The phone rings, and it's my mom. Ok, now 30 minutes have passed, and I realize time is flying. I have to finish my task. I hang up the phone with mom and start cleaning the kitchen because this is where I answered the phone. This was the room I was currently in. Wrong! I have not started to create order. I have caused my mind to create chaos. Yes, chaos. Because I can't remember if I cleaned the bathroom floor or not, and now I am on this kick to finish the kitchen.

38

Get Your Stuff
In Order

This is where those baby steps come into play. It would be better to go back to the bathroom and finish that task to create order. When I reached the bathroom I would know what I have cleaned and what needs to be finished. I know some of you just said, "No, it would have been better not to answer the phone call from mom." Ok, maybe you're right, but this is my book.

Anyway, then I could go back to the kitchen and start to create order there and finish the kitchen which will give me a feeling of productivity…a great way to lift my spirit because I have established order. Are you getting the picture?

There are so many areas where order is required in our life…to help balance us out and make us feel like good achievers. Areas from your health are: eating proper foods, good nutrition, and exercise programs. Other areas are: your family, your friendships, your marriage, and your finances.

Order may need to start with your walk with God: spending time in prayer, singing and rejoicing for how far you have already come…not complaining on how you need to get further. Just relax in God's timing. With your obedience to His word and being honest about yourself and your relationship with Him, you'll get there. Order may need to start at work: filing papers, finishing a project you've held off for weeks, or maybe even in establishing the right relationships with people.

People are like elevators. They will take you up or take you down. That will either multiply, divide, or subtract from your life. Who you hang around with is a signal of what you will become, and where you are going. Please, please have right connections. People are vital to creating order. Some will

People are like elevators… they will take you up or take you down.

encourage and lift your spirits, while others may tear you apart and bury you in discouragement. You choose, and be led by God for the right connections.

I have just listed a few areas that are basically common among all of us. I am sure the list goes on and on, because each one of us is different and has different responsibilities to handle, and different personalities. In all of these differences, we are all unique in our own special way, created by God for His glory and created in His image. So keeping this in mind, I will leave the areas of order you need to change in you or start up, to you.

My job is to give you information to enhance what you know, remind you of something you forget, help you see another perspective, or just to help you understand. I hope in this small chapter (yet it could have become a very detailed one) you have found an area you need to start with to create order in your life. I just wanted to give you a small taste of how-sweet-it-is when order is achieved. Hopefully, some creative juices are flowing for you. *Now, stop neglecting and start creating!*

Spoil
Yourself

EIGHT WAYS
to Lift
YOUR *Spirit*

CHAPTER FIVE

I think taking time for you is important for your personal well being. I talk to countless people throughout my travels around the world, and I have found a common denominator among most of them. That is "Time." "Never enough time to finish a task...If only there were 48 hours in one day...Who has time to relax and enjoy the scenery?" This is what I often hear along with "Boy, if I had just five minutes to regroup, ten minutes for the newspaper. Oh, how I would love to take a bath and relax, see a movie, read a book." My response often is, "Who's stopping you?" I get a funny glare and confused eyes that stare back at me and say, "No one, but me."

If it's going to be, it is up to me. I have found that no one can truly dictate to you, your schedule, but you. Of course, we need to get guidance from God on His plans for our life. It is vital to daily put Him first and spend time in His presence before your day even starts. This is your responsibility. So if you have slacked off, take advice from Chapter Four and start creating order by spending time with God. I do understand that we all have responsibilities, jobs, family, special functions to attend, church, etc.... What I don't understand is why haven't you scheduled time for YOU in the midst of it all? Do you really think you can effectively give out when you have made no deposits? This would be silly to think.

I will help give you a few suggestions on "down time." It is very important to recharge your human battery. Even cars don't run without gas. Children need food to grow, and adults need down time to go. Life's system is a cycle. Look at the butterfly before it flies. It was in a cocoon. It had down time regardless. It couldn't fly until this metamorphosis process took place. We should take a tiny lesson from this. Regardless of what goes on in our life, we must rest, *relax*. Metamorphosis means, 1) change of physical form, structure, or substance especially by supernatural means; 2) a striking alteration in appearance, character, or circumstances. When we have rest, it shows. When we have taken the time to become rejuvenated, others notice it as well. Look at the second part of the definition, striking alteration in appearance, character, or *circumstance*. Self-explanatory, isn't it? Our outlook changes during this process. Call it what you may. Just take time to enjoy life so you look better to others as well as yourself.

If your feeling frazzled, you're getting too little sleep, running here and there, too many expectations, and too many of "you" required in too many places. Take time out for yourself! It's ok. Even God rested on the seventh day. Learn to appreciate the five to ten minutes of solace you may get throughout your day. Embrace it and don't think about another thing other than relaxation. I do hope you take more than five minutes though. I am just using this as an example. R&R — relax and rejuvenate...or the traditional rest and recuperation. I don't think it's often a matter of recouping that we need. However, more of the matter of rejuvenating is needed to pick us back up to lift our spirits. In this day and age, demands are high and so is stress. So we must take time to de-stress by using the R&R method.

Don't wait until you are at the end of your rope (the edge of exhaustion) before you take R&R. Learn to seize the moment during your day. At lunch breaks, slip away to a quiet place. This is a time when you're allowed to alienate yourself from the world. Remember no one is going to tell you to take time out other than you. Besides, we make children do this. Where along the line did we forget to make ourselves follow this same rule?

What you believe will create your circumstance. If you believe you have no time, then you won't. If you believe that time is all you have, then you have to use it wisely…even if it is to take R&R. Then you will be wise with time. The choices in life are all up to us. We want to blame others for the way we feel or for the lack of time we do have when we shape our days by our daily habits. Choose life. Even the Bible states in John 10:10, *"The thief cometh not but for to steal, and to kill, and to destroy: I am come that they might have 'life,' and that they might have it more abundantly."* God wants us to have life. He required for us to choose it. He also required for us to rest. So what is the delay? Tomorrow is not here yet. So enjoy today on your way to tomorrow. Take no thought for tomorrow for tomorrow will take care of itself. All we ever have is today because when we get to tomorrow, we'll just rename it today. So choose life today!

Let me give you a few suggestions to help you gain R&R, and then the rest is up to you.

After a long day at the office, and you return to your home your haven, don't answer the phone if you don't want to. They are calling you, remember? They obviously want to talk, but do you

44

You be the judge here, I know when I need to answer my phone, and when I don't.

Keep a journal of your daily progress, your thoughts. Writing often helps you release what is bottled up inside or even enhances what's in there. You have no one to judge you when you write (unless you pass your words onto someone else). It is just you and your journal. Find a quiet place to go and write. This may even help you when you look back in a week or a year from now to see how far you've come…in turn giving you strength and rejuvenating you.

8 Ways to To Rest and Relax

1 ▶ Walk around the mall just for fun! This is one particular habit of rest for me. My husband says that I may get a lot of rest, but his wallet doesn't. Seriously, just learn to window shop. It can relax the mind and tone up your body at the same time. You can do it…without spending. I am still learning to master that one.

2 ▶ Walk down memory lane. Take out old photos of you or your family and reminisce of the fun times and places you've experienced.

3 ▶ Bubble baths (yes, men, you can take them, too, I won't tell). Take the phone off the hook, put on some soothing music, (maybe even light some candles) and soothe your stress away.

4 ▶ Schedule a lunch date — maybe with an old friend or someone close to you and eat at the nicest restaurant that is affordable to you. Go ahead treat yourself.

Spoil Yourself

5 ICE CREAM-YOU SCREAM — we all scream for ice cream. Allow yourself one day to indulge in great fatting food! (And don't complain about how gross you may feel afterwards. Just don't make cheating on junk foods a habit. Remember this is for R&R).

6 Rent a movie – and just "veg out" at home all night.

7 Just say, "NO!" You don't have to accept every invite or opportunity. The more time you save, the more R&R you'll have. And the more you'll effectively give of yourself to others.

8 Visit a nursing home and give of yourself for a few hours. You'll feel a great sense of uplifting knowing you selflessly gave to another human being.

46

These are only a few ideas for you to follow. Maybe you can create your own and pass them on to others. Whatever you do, realize how important it is to use your time to your advantage to regroup, and relax, and rejuvenate in order to lift your spirit.

Here is a positive confession for you:

I choose today to make the most of my day, to put God first, and to live an abundant life. If I lack in an area, I am honest with myself in ways I can improve. I will take action in the areas to enhance myself and lift my mental well being. I will not be mean to myself and neglect the time I need to be refreshed and give out to others. I choose to take R&R (relax & rejuvenate) time to lift my spirit, and I will not interrupt my R&R time with silly reasons of why I don't deserve rest. God also rested on the seventh day. If it is going to be, it's up to me.

Mirror, Mirror
On the Wall

CHAPTER SIX

Mirror, Mirror On the Wall

The eye is a very powerful tool in which we gain much perspective, because how we view something or interpret things is often determined by what we see. How do you see yourself? Do you see yourself through the eyes of God, or do you have a poor self-image? Do you see the God who created you, or do you see what others think about you?

Only you can be honest and answer these questions with clarity. It is important to see yourself the way God sees you. You were created in His image and likeness. You are the finest thing that God has ever created! You are God's favorite child, and He cares so very much about you.

How you see yourself makes a world of difference because when you see the good in you, you attract more good. I want you to understand the value of what you see, and how it can affect or defect you. I don't want to focus on the bad things, but I want you to focus on seeing the greatness you possess, the abilities that lay in the very fibers of your soul. I want you to see yourself in the mirror and appreciate who you are.

I will give you practical application types that will help you achieve this goal and increase your ability to lift your spirits. I want you to be totally aware of all the uniqueness you hold and how honored others are to be in your presence, all through the power of the eye. You should qualify your time and who you allow to be a part of it. Remember Chapter Four? The people you surround yourself with can bring you up or pull you down. You *can* achieve greatness and see yourself through the eyes of God. See yourself in the future full of God's goodness and grace. You must act as if it is impossible to fail at achieving this goal as you read. It really is achievable. It's just up to you.

When you change your mind about you, everyone and everything around you changes. Take some time out to do a self-evaluation. What do you see? Go to the mirror and evaluate your responses. Mirror, Mirror, who am I? What is the image you see of yourself? Is it positive or negative? Do you feel discouraged or uplifted?

You know, for years I saw a damaged, barely surviving, skinny, brown- haired, blue-eyed girl. I saw a defeated, miserable girl that was worthy of nothing. I saw a girl who thought she was unlovable, and in turn did not know how to love. I saw a girl in search of herself; and as this journey prolonged, she only found other areas of insignificance and showed hatred toward her own body. I saw a girl that no one wanted and everyone made fun of, a girl who wasn't an "A" student, nor was she a spunky cheerleader. All I saw was defeat and low self-esteem. This girl was me!

From a young teenage girl, I battled with such low self-esteem…so bad to the point where I would put bruises on my own body. I would look in the mirror and beat myself up. I would hit myself hard and pull my hair till it would come out of my head and into my hands. I talked negativity all the time over my life. I was in desperate search of some significance. I really needed Jesus, and His love, to transform and lift my life. Then one day my eyes were opened, I saw myself in a new light. I saw, for the first time, a girl who found a friend and this friend became her significance. His name is Jesus.

No, I didn't get there overnight. I remember times when I didn't know how to improve, but my heart was willing for someone to help. My head just didn't know how to do this. I started with the small things. I started to look at myself in the mirror and appreciate what I saw, and I began to ask myself questions. Questions like, *"What don't I like about what I see? Why? How can I change what I don't like? Did Jesus create me?* Yes...then I really can't be that bad after all!" I realized then, I was all right. From this point on I began to repeat that I liked myself over and over until it sunk deep into my soul, and my mind just automatically believed this truth. *What you continually hear, you will eventually believe.*

This is a process that came by my faith and by the knowledge that I gained in knowing God created this cute package, and everything He created was good. So for months and months I would stand in front of the mirror and proclaim positive confessions over my life. Then when it began to sink in, I started to write down on paper how I felt about me. There were post-it-notes everywhere, but hey, whatever works! I began to study and read what God's Word said about things He created. I would post scriptures on my mirror and read them daily to continually remind myself.

One day, before I knew it, my mind was rejuvenated. My heart felt happy again, and my spirits were lifted all because of the power of what I saw. I was able to see that I was created in God's image. I finally grasped that God saw me as made in His image! For me that was enough. I just had to believe this truth and practice the power of what I saw, and then learn to receive strength, change, mercy, love and grace. It was a process. But, I finally got there.

Yes, from time to time I am tempted in this area. I battle with everyday people and their defeating words, and I try hard not to allow them to take root in my heart. When this does occur, I go to God's Word to find out what He says about me. I surround myself with positive people and then just say, "I love me!" Like I said before, it is a process. But, your spirits will be uplifted when you put your mouth and your heart to God's Word, and then just do what it says. The joy and reality of the greatness of who you really are comes to light!

I challenge you to start looking in the mirror! Learn to like a few things about yourself. Then, work your way until you can love what you see. The thing is to be honest with yourself, and then let God do the rest with your obedient heart and willingness to improve. Also, it would be helpful if you made daily confessions. Below are a few points to get you started on this routine. Please, don't stop there. Couple it with God's Word, and watch what you see. SEE GREATNESS ALL OVER YOU!

What you say, you will eventually believe:

- ▶ God sees me as a strong and courageous person.
- ▶ God sees me as an intelligent person.
- ▶ I am created in the image and likeness of God.
- ▶ God sees me as a person full of potential.
- ▶ God knows the real me, and He loves me.
- ▶ I am blessed, and I am on my way to victory.

Begin to create an awareness of who you really are and hold your head up high. Square your shoulders back, and walk like a child of the King! Because God cares for you. He tells us in His word to cast all our cares on Him. So what are you waiting for? Cast all your fears, worries, doubts, anxieties...everything. Don't hold back!

"Peace I leave with you, my peace I give unto you: not as the world giveth, give I unto you. Let not your heart be troubled, neither let it be afraid."
(JOHN 14:27)

Jesus has given us ways to appropriate His peace in our life. Here's a little homework for you. Get your Bible and look up Psalm 94:19 and Psalm 119:165. Continue to feed your spirit with these scriptures. They will help you stay in peace, not in pieces! Resist the devil, and he will flee from you. Lay aside every weight of the world, and allow your sprit to soar into new heights through the grace and mercy of God.

Seasons
Change

CHAPTER SEVEN

Seasons Change

To everything there is a time and a season.

irst of all, you have to realize that no condition is permanent. There are seasons in your life just as in nature. No storm that you face will last, remember it soon shall pass. The important thing to know is that in the midst of change, it is possible to be happy. It is possible for your spirits to be lifted. So get happy. Change is inevitable, but misery is optional!

I know the importance of planning. I believe in it, but I am careful not to plan too far ahead. Some will tell you that you need one-year, five-year and ten-year goals. The Japanese have 100-year goals.

Myself, I do not usually plan farther ahead than one year. Many things can happen in a year. The seasons change, and therefore my plans have to change. You must be prepared for change, or you will never succeed. One of the greatest books that I have read on change is the book, *Who Moved my Cheese?* by Spencer Johnson. I encourage you to invest in your future and buy a copy.

If you can discover how to successfully deal with change, you will be able to enjoy life. You will experience less stress and more success in your work and in your life. Your spirits will be lifted through the reality of facing change. Here are a few things that will help you to understand change:

Change Happens.
You might as well be ready for it. If you do not change, you will become extinct.

Anticipate Change.
Be ready to move on.

Monitor Change.
Know what is happening around you. What's new?

Adapt to change quickly.
The quicker you let go of the past, the sooner you can enjoy the future. Notice small changes early, and it will help you adapt to bigger changes when they come.

Change.
Move! Do something! It is better and safer to change than to remain in the desert of what use to work.

Enjoy Change.
Get excited about the adventure. When you move beyond fear, to that place of faith, you will feel free.

Be ready to change quickly and enjoy it again and again. Keep moving! The quicker you let go of what use to work, the sooner you can enjoy the benefits of what is working today.

Enjoy today on your way to tomorrow. Celebrate change, but don't become a know it all in the process. I feel sorry for the person who becomes prideful on their chain of accomplishments. They begin to think that nothing can happen to them, and when the storm hits, they are not prepared, and they lose everything. This will not lift your spirits but only bury them. Prepare for change.

I know of people who get stuck in a stream of failure after failure. Soon they quit trying. They give up right at the time the season was changing in their favor and success was reaching out to embrace them. Never stop trying! Crisis is always at the curve of a change.

Know that the conditions will change. Hold on! Don't give up! Don't grow weary in well doing for in due SEASON you will reap, if you faint not. Just as you know the sun will rise again, so you also can know that this season of misfortune must end. It was always so, and it will always be.

Now if your work, your patience and your goals have brought you success, look for someone who is in an off-season and lift him or her up. This is preparing for your future. The day will come, according to Ephesians 6:8, that what you make happen for another, God will make happen for you. Help lift the spirits of someone else today!

Observation

When change occurs I have a choice. I choose to react in a healthy way by:

_____

_____

_____

_____

_____

_____

Get Your Directions From Upstairs

CHAPTER EIGHT

Get Your Directions From Upstairs

When all is said and done, you must know in your heart that your direction came from the heartbeat of God. You have heard His voice for direction in your life. There is a joy and certainty that will come and lift your spirit when you know you are exactly where God wants you. You are in the right place, at the right time.

Open your heart's door and allow your spirits to be lifted when you surrender yourself to the will of God. He knows the thoughts and plans for your life anyway. He created you, and He knows exactly what you need to get you to the next level. So what are you waiting for? Develop a healthy relationship with God and get his directions for your life.

Getting direction is easy. We complicate it and make excuses as to why we can't receive it. When you need to go on an interview, or to the new mall, or a new restaurant and don't know how to get there don't you stop and ask for directions? Gotcha! I knew it. You took the time to find out where your destination was. Do the same thing with God. Just stop and ask directions for your destination and don't make excuses. Oh, I don't have time. I have too much to do, too many projects, the children, the boss, the husband, the deadlines etc.... Stop making excuses for why you are in a rut. Just make time. It is that easy. God wants you to talk to Him. He created you, and He wants your spirits to be lifted. It would just be helpful if you included Him in the daily decisions of your life.

God cannot communicate with you about your life if you ignore Him. So don't complain about what you permit. Do not ignore God — trust me. Do you want to live happy and free, full of joy and peace? Then talk to God. It is that simple, just talk to Him like you talk to your friend. Yep! It is that easy! Try it. If your mind is weak and your spirits are down in the dumps, give God a try. You have nothing to lose, do you? God only has the ability to make our lives better through constant communion with Him. He knows no lack because He holds the answer to abundance. He knows no oppression, because He holds the answer to peace. He doesn't know doubt, because He is the author of faith.

Wake up! Get refreshed! Renew and lift your spirit! Get your directions from upstairs. Talk to God! HOW? Just open your mouth as I mentioned before. God isn't impressed with your fancy speech and traditional rituals. He just wants to chat. Let me give you a little key to help — CLEAN UP FIRST.

What do I mean? Well, if you had a special meeting or an interview (just an example) wouldn't you get showered, put on nice clothes and make yourself presentable? Without looking presentable, you may not feel your best, the most alert or confident. Would you go to an important interview in pajamas? It's doubtful! Care enough about yourself that others will take interest. The same is with God. If you need direction, go to Him prepared. Your spirit will automatically be lifted because your mind is first lifted, and your image is confident. The power of what you see changes.

That's right! Go shower! Clean up! Put on cute, clean, comfy clothes! Fix yourself up and go on your interview with God. Go get your directions from upstairs. Get out of the basement of gloom, despair and agony and talk to God for your answer! You must be at your best. Your mind must be fresh and new. Now, I know, sometimes it is difficult to clean up if you are feeling down, discouraged and unworthy. However, cleaning up is necessary for your own good. It will change your perception of your circumstances. You can do it! Use the power of the eye and create order in yourself. Remember, it's all up to you. Then go upstairs for your meeting.

God is waiting. Shut the door! Turn the phones off! Put the dog in the room and start to chat with God. If you want something you've never had, you're going to have to do something you've never done. All the power to change is up to you. The ability to lift your spirits is just the ability to take action to make it happen. So with enough said, I am signing off to let you chat with God. Meditate on the things you've read in this book, and soon you'll see your spirits will be lifted. You can do it! Just make the decision and go for it.

Observation
The directions I need most today are:

_____

_____

_____

_____

_____

_____

"God has my answers.
I need to get my direction from Him everyday."

The ways I plan on getting directions are:

_____ 61

_____

_____

_____

_____

_____

Believing in you,
Christine Martin

Get Your Directions From Upstairs

Additional Material by Christine Martin

The Resurrected Woman

This 4-tape, audio series is packed with powerful secrets on how to pick yourself up and win!

$30.00

Motivate Yourself

Do you need a jumpstart? This 4-tape, audio series will teach you how to enhance and transform your life.

$30.00

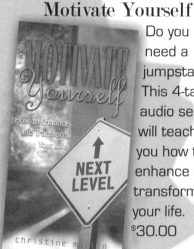

Order online at www.christinemartin.org or by calling 407.445.0506